NEAR SCATTERED PRAISE LIES OUR SUBSTANTIAL ENDEAVOR

11/14/22

To Lakeisha,

A wonderful person whom I love dearly! Please enjoy these poems!

Ron

Ron Penoyer

NEAR SCATTERED PRAISE LIES OUR SUBSTANTIAL ENDEAVOR

Collected Poems

atmosphere press

Published by Atmosphere Press

Cover design by Ronaldo Alves

atmospherepress.com

To Patricia A. Newton, M.D., as promised

In memory of Philip Booth

CONTENTS

ONE
Ante Meridiem

TWO
Post Meridiem

Fragments and Petites Essais

AUTHOR'S NOTE

Over a period of decades I have sought to write poems that take reasoned, and perhaps reasonable, risks or liberties with the conventions of poetry as I have known them in my lifetime. My efforts have taken place from roughly the mid-1960s, when I developed a love of writing poetry and an appreciation for what I might call poetic sensibility. During the second half of the 1960s I was fortunate to be encouraged briefly in my writing by the late poet Philip Booth, whose great spirit and generosity I honor here and to whom I owe a debt of gratitude. Admittedly, the risks to which I refer were, and are, minor compared to the extreme and comprehensive efforts of many other writers. In my case, those liberties were frequently motivated by impatience and frustration with – perhaps even a lack of respect for – what I considered to be the tired and tiresome conventions of rhyme, form, diction, themes and other features of poetry as taught to me from a young age. Over time, I have also been interested in writing poems that are, in subtle or obvious ways, deeply and inherently different but do not *look* different. It is a matter of debate whether or not I have succeeded.

The poems in this collection are divided into three parts. To some extent, the first two divisions are intended to be artificial in nature. But – most definitely – the poems in the first part, "Ante Meridiem," are separated from those in the second part, "Post Meridiem," by a period in my life when I (belatedly) reached what I will call a "noon" in my understanding of the survival of my spirit. In particular, that period was marked by life-threatening events that continue to present challenges to me as I write this. The third section contains what I call "petites essais," with humble acknowledgement of the French for "trial" or "attempt" – in my case on an exceedingly small scale – to understand fundamental truths that I believe are often hidden in minimal words.

These poems are, at least, a record of time and thought spent in survival. Only a small handful of them have seen the light of day, in publication, before now. I prefer that my reasons for not wishing to publish poems in literary journals and magazines, or elsewhere, remain private. But it is true that I developed, years ago, wariness about the company I keep and, by extension, the company my poems keep. This wariness increased as tastes in poetry continued to change markedly (particularly in recent years). I am certain that many, if not all, publishers of poetry are equally particular about the guests they invite into their pages, though it would seem that many display few scruples in that regard.

Overall, in presenting this collection, I believe there is value in offering poems that stimulate and demand deep thought and consideration of ideas and emotions, ideally in ways that are mysterious, surprising, delightful, sometimes amusing, and perhaps time-delayed, like a depth-charge that must reach a certain place in dark waters before it detonates. These effects may be accomplished with words, phrases, lines and forms that, at first, may seem nonsensical, contradictory, unreal, bizarre or meaningless. I offer these poems with the intention and hope that great meaning, great emotion and great understanding may be discovered and accomplished through each of these.

June 2022
Creve Coeur, Missouri

ONE
Ante Meridiem

"Thomas wished he had been able to do this as a writer, find a tone or a context that was beyond himself, that was rooted in what shone and glittered and could be seen, but that hovered above the world of fact, entering into a place where spirit and substance could merge and drift apart and merge again."

-- Colm Tóibín, *The Magician*

BELIEF

It's raining as I write this.
I'm telling you the truth:
you can hear the rain on the roof,
an insistent splattering sound.

The sound of rain is the truth.
If you were here you'd hear it,
you'd know it must be true,
right as rain, good and true.

You'd see it wash the windows
and the window screens, watch it
carve streams in the driveway,
see it revive itself as a rainbow.

I'm not lying: I'm not that boy
in Aesop who cried about a wolf.
This is about the rain, and belief
in the rain. Not a boy, not a wolf.

Now you can hear it stop.

CROSSING: COVERED BRIDGE

the second time I ever crossed one
it was with you nowhere
and boards below rattled weakly
as though dry old men
who'd grown up with us
who'd supported us one by one
now were tired of such favors

this side's the same as the other
but our direction's changed
we've been sheltered for no reason
a roof passed over us
its pretext for being is quaint
water went under and carried
our other bank with it

I see your face your second nature
but the first was just
as familiar to my moving eyes
you steer and bring the sun
round to your side of the wheel
I have seen that light
from a different side of day

and I have loved you even
though tired old men rattled
their weary trappings at us
while you've brought the light
so many ways around me
and the water has carried
so much behind us away

ON NEARING THE ISLE OF ITHACA

The water that will not move
is a cesspool muddied by the continents;
the ship that came, in blindness,
is now a wreck on a broken beach.
To this island Odysseus had hoped to come
when work and duty elsewhere had ended,
when sidetracked travels were over at last.
But an island can't draw maps for those
who long to reach it. Journeyers
must learn to face risks in coming,
must see that all routes are blind.

The water clouds in higher billows,
the sky is rinsed with darker grays.
Ships anchored in choked seaweed
have sighed for a sight of that
always-sought isle, have yearned for
rudders that would not fail in the
slightest storms. On silent shores
their prows now slump in the knowledge
that the kingdom that has already come
will be there, also, long afterward. . . .
But the oarsmen, for one instant, missed
the crucial beat. Once beached,

even crystal waters can't lure the oars.

DOING LAUNDRY

Working from the backward end
I look into the bright intestines,
the whirling guts waterclogged with cotton.
Sun pours in after rain,
autumn having dampened the spirits
made drunk in lonely rooms,
and the digestive sloshing sound
suspends itself around tables
where books are stacked on emptiness.
I ask, what of tomorrow's diluted suds
poured through clear chlorination,
tumbled-dried in August's after-air?
I hear what time has said in its minutes
and hours, the drops of rain
churned through hourglass clouds
in the pressures of atmosphere.
The air, bookbound with emptiness;
Gothic windows, hazed in clichés;
the night, whispered into sleeping ears.

I know the cycles eventually stop,
the water drains, the cotton wrinkles.
But water, dissolving into sunshine,
drips from the curves and myriad edges
of this backward end -- unbearable loads
pouring forth a superficial saturation,
the old water continually turning
into and onto the sound of itself.

GIFT

(for D.B.B.)

You came bearing leaves from autumn,
tramping through the snow, from a tree
which, even now, in February's freeze,
bore shriveled foliage as winter decoration.
It wasn't much, or perhaps too much:
something from an autumn we had lived through,
something left behind like rabbit tracks
in crusted snow, leading away.

Lilacs on a branch flashed through my mind
rabbit-like, redolent with a fragrance
I could smell for an instant, then no more.
Time passed through time – a track
retraced, an old path retraveled,
an instant swiftly relived. . . .

You came bearing leaves, while the sun
began to sink into a deeper cold.
The tree stood shadowed against
a yellowed sky, clumped here and there
with adamant leaves the wind had found
imperturbable, impervious to force.
We stood there, with leaves in gloves that
shielded us, and watched the snuffed-out sun
smoke into a twilight that took us home
through tracks we'd tramped in coming there.

TOMMASO DE'CAVALIERI

The mornings are the trials
Of our yearnings and beginnings.
In the naked realm of the earthly,
The celestial only begins to arise,
Like a heavenly glow attempting
To pierce a host of leaden clouds.
But the Titan has made you thus,
And has loved you; he yet does.

The art of awakening has begun,
As shadows make complex patterns
On the bleakness of our western wall.
Love alone is the judge at our trial,
As earth's fierce storms rage on and on . . .
And the sun rejects the shadow.

FOX

the chase can never
trap it up a tree.
time is too shrewd.
frosted autumns that freeze
into winters keep finding
the old animal curled up
in some niche of its nature,
bleary-eyed but alert.
we who chew on bones
haven't the sense to realize
the vanity of perseverance:
the fox is but a chimera,
evanescent as a breeze,
furry and fleeting
like scatterings of snow
in deep January,
blizzard-beset.
in the end, what we do
is settle down, yawn and
lick our forepaws, consoling
ourselves with the contentment
of having chased, having
scared the devil through
piles of leaves, to winter away
our run-for-the-money . . .
until the spring comes.

APPLE TREES

It is urgent that you know
The trees on my street, on my way to work,
Have burst into bloom – a huge new vista,
Tree after tree, a long streak of blossoms.

In a spring emergency, the April soil
Beneath the sidewalks sent
An electric charge to barren limbs,
Enlivening, startling them to overdrive.

(I hear them dreaming of apples.)

It is urgent that you know
This pink and white extravagance
Burst from unassuming trees
Is more than I can bear or comprehend.

This morning, entering the world, unbelieving,
Expecting no change of season, no reason
For hope or joy, suddenly the earth
Has changed, the world is blooming.

DIET OF WORMS

The mice in our walls are screaming.
I've never heard such a sound, except
That time when Auntie Marg went crazy.
Her son, my cousin, joined the Army.

In Vietnam he joined the dead.
Nobody paid attention. Our men
Disappeared in jungles and we said
We'd never listen to barking Generals again.

So now the rats in our alleys are shouting
Like nothing I've known in this life,
Slogans I can barely translate, rife
With resentment and darkness and lies.

Demented Luthers, huddling in hunger,
These frantic vermin nail their agendas
On every loosened door – insistent, certain,
Demanding. And when they scatter,

they scatter in glee, in wonder.

ADVICE

I heard you out
and now
I have nothing to say.
I assent,
automatic puppet
yessing
from a parched throat,
nodding
like a fat alcoholic
skirting sleep.

Decisions bustle past me
with neat signatures.

From now on
I have nothing to say.
I have heard you out,
I still hear you out
a thousand times
each night.

In my nightmares
whole futures
settle in your voice,
cackling over
cracked eggs.

PENANCE

The light in the bedroom,
The bedroom bright with darkness,
The bed an immaculate sin.

You are not listening to me,
You are not listening to all
I'm not saying.

You punctuate a first draft
Of coffee with silence;
Your forehead studies its furrows.

On your wall hang men
You've left on hold, faces
Framed in small confessionals.

You are not listening to me,
You are adrift in your smoke,
Your fingers glow into ashes.

I could say, close the door
I dread going through;
I could say, pull the shade.

The light in your bedroom,
The darkness in the bed,
Faces bright in the darkness.

Frozen in still poses, I see
Your men repenting, I see the wall
Crack with their punishments.

I am hearing you imagine me
Saying what I want; I am wanting
You to hear me say what I imagine:

The light in the bedroom,
The bedroom circled with darkness,
The circle filled with all

You can hear me not saying,
Unsayable, never said,
Never needing to say.

STONEHENGE

Stars in the last moments of evening
twist and twinkle out blind prophecies,
no different than on primal nights when
whirling constellations went by Celtic names.

Stones, to what you stand no one knows,
nor does it seem to matter – not to Parliament
or the Queen, far from Wiltshire plains and
butterscotch moons rising high in summer.

Strange forces surely must have driven
Druid engineers to such extremes with
these rocks, an urge of gods or devils crazed
by a punctual sun arising at equinox.

Secrets prevail, and not a single wise man
from tourist buses can add an ounce of
meaning to this place, nor a single cubit
to the stature of these petrified goliaths.

Sarcen stones, tall megaliths, empty
doorways without walls, lean and face
each other, as if to ask what could be
the hollow myth that haunts this starlit place.

So who or what but the zodiac, or an almanac
of the ages, will write on heaven or earth
an answer? Words are as blind as
silent stars, as cold as chiseled stone.

COUNTDOWN

T minus 60 seconds
and counting
marbles on 4th Street
which Joey collected
since age 5½
years ago the
buildings were new
but now they're
falling down to
T minus 50
on the Cape
and all systems are go
up the street
to Stuyvesant which
is the end of the
world and beyond
it are monsters breathing
jet propulsion fuel
now disconnected from
the pad at T minus 40
all systems are green
light at the corner
by the delicatessen
where meat is grown
in white wax paper
and milk is made in
bottles like the ones
Daddy brings home to the
pad now cleared at
T minus 30 while voice
communications with
the world through the
welfare worker are not
proceeding at T minus
20 and now removed
from the launching room
are 2 dead rats and
Mamma is screaming
10, 9, 8, 7 days till
the next check comes for

6, 5, 4, 3 dollars or even
2, 1, Zero, Ignition, Lift-Off
to buy a pair of brand
new shining rockets.

FIREFLIES

"Mehr licht" – Johann Wolfgang von Goethe

Meticulous, manicured lawns swept
With bursts of light, disturbing night
By questioning the dark, pondering
Substance, snared by absence of light.

(Fireflies could be the death of us.)

Light or night? Go figure. Insects
Will rule what's left of the world!
A bright exclamation in darkness
Cancels meaning, snuffs precious light.

(Precious? Light? Prove that.)

The thought, the poem, will end here,
As fireflies incite, ignite the night
(Ignite themselves) against deep dark.
An onlooker, I seek more light.

(More light. To seek more light.)

Measured, marvelous lawns – swept
With inexplicable light, defiance of night,
Sporadic questions, holding the dark as
Suspended substance, unbelievably bright.

(Hold the darkness, hold the terrible light!)

DIAGNOSIS

Christmas 2004

You'll wake one morning to find your house
has been rearranged, the bed now faces
east not west, the sun pours through
the wrong window, you've lost the fireplace.

You'll stare in the bathroom mirror and see
the cancer standing in your skin, a stranger
inhabiting your flesh, claiming your body,
drugging your brain, too friendly with danger.

You will not panic, you'll calmly step
outside the riddle of your human being,
gasping the simple air, and occupy a place
where believing is requisite to seeing.

You'll give it time, it gives you no such thing.
Laughing out loud at reason, it does not care
what your life has meant till now, and winks
when it hears your world burst into prayer.

GOSPEL TRUTH

Christmas 2013

The story we're told is
a story, we're told,
something old,
not necessarily
trustworthy, a little fast
and loose with the truth,
fuzzy at the edges.
Several accounts
don't even recount
the central event;
not a word.
What's missing prevents us
from avoiding distress
at what we've heard.
When we question the part
about the stable and manger,
the story line hedges.
It sounds like a fable.
But the gaps attest
to what's left unsaid:
the danger of using the head
for a story told to the heart.

EXPEDITION

Christmas 2014

It doesn't matter
about the weather,
whether sun or rain or snow
follow us when we go
into the woods to hunt
the one incomparable tree.
Spruce and pine and fir
are barely distinguishable
when what we're looking for
isn't the tree itself.
A beautiful shape's a plus,
the right height ameliorates
its standing in the house,
but our spirits don't require
a perfect earthly thing
to decorate tonight:
what we're seeking is
the light.

DELIVERY

Christmas 2015

FedEx trucks and Big Brown vans
criss-cross at every intersection.
I brake and wait for lights
that regulate mid-December traffic.
Behind the wheel impatience reigns.

Commerce is the king of streets
and parking lots at Gallerias
built to satisfy earthly whims
and stoke acquisitive fires.
Getting is the drug in our veins.

Or maybe not. City Hall's evergreen
is modestly attired in lights –
red, green, white, some blue.
At its height a star makes do
as a beacon of transcendence.

Past the suburbs, interstates
narrow down to county roads.
Fields accommodate herds of cattle
and winter wheat. A barn reminds
a stranger of work he needs to do.

In the loft I smell the rich, forgiving hay.

WREATH

Christmas 2017

The wreath on the door is evergreen,
or so we say.

But sooner rather than later
comes a day the pine needles

fall away, meet their maker.
Nothing protects it.

The wreath's circle seems eternal,
a proxy for long life,

sign of a world without end.
But instead, its season passes,

and the door, unadorned,
is strictly an exit.

THE LINDEN TREE

Christmas 2018

Even this late in the year
leaves cling to the linden tree.
Their tenacity is nearer than near.
I, too, have budded and leafed
in the shade of this aging tree,
but how have I lived through this year?

How will this tree, in time,
reawaken to synthesize light –
light now broken in shards
in this winter-desert yard?
What if it fails to flourish in spring?
How do I live through this fear?

Have I taken the blessing of life,
the wild-guessing of my pulse,
the lessening of years –
have I taken them to heart?
Have I taken my heart to heart?
Have I learned from the leaf and the tree?

AT WINTER SOLSTICE

Christmas 2019

O wide, unending night
O hidden spring of light

the snow tonight
is an imagined thing

that counters darkness
with examined sight.

I will fall asleep
and breathe at last

under fragrant trees
where time is deep

and even the past
takes mercy on me.

O vast, unending night
O nearest stream of light

may the broken souls
of those I've lost and grieve

sleep with me here
under fragrant trees

and be made whole.

EVEN IN EDEN

Christmas 2020

Even in Eden, Adam
and his rib-mate Eve
likely mourned the loss
of an earlier paradise
from which they were tossed;

shook their fists at a god
who curtailed their bliss
and masked the meaning
of strictures and warnings.
They had no scripture
to inform them of risks.

Surely they met
a feckless snake,
or a reckless bat,
or microscopic gnats
that tore their world apart
with perfect treachery;

surely, among the ruins,
they sat with each other,
in their grief and pain,
with disease, and death,
and their broken hearts,

and started their lives
over again.

LOOKING FOR MEANING

Christmas 2021

Looking for meaning
in the indifferent fact
of metastasis
will disappoint
the heart and mind
every time –
or, perhaps,
shed more light
on meaning-
lessness.

Less can be said
about seeking an end
to the wild spread
of lambent cells
that know no bounds
and couldn't care less
about carelessness
or the subtle fall
of hopefulness.

Looking for meaning
isn't a job
that soothes the soul
or befits the end
of one's days.
It trolls the truth:
The days themselves
are the meaning.

THINGS I PROMISED TO DO

Climb the stairs with a Valentine.
Comb your hair with a porcupine.

Protest that you are out of order.
Write lyrics for something by Porter.

Free the Muse who made me a slave.
Read Plato in an Aegean cave.

Season our losses with sprigs of time.
Take umbrage with confounding rhyme.

Somehow imagine the unimaginable.
Believe that your heart is attainable.

AN UGLY THING

In bright
sub-freezing sunlight
an ugly thing
wanders across
the dark asphalt
of the courtyard.

A tottering young
opossum's got
some nerve to think
it's safe to forage
in broad daylight.

When I draw near
its eyes become
hypnotized

as if ancient fear
and the delusional grip
of immobility

could fool the world
or change
its fate.

THE HOMERIC LIFE FOR ME

Critics plow their fields,
argue over wine-dark seas,
yearn to be ancient minstrels
or ancient mariners –
Homeric, epic,
epochal, Odyssean.

Hanging at home
won't attract the girls.

In purple groves of academe
tipsy students uncork
Château Mont-Redon
with their sharp feral teeth
to prove intestinal fortitude,
to publish or
perish the thought
of frat boys as captains
of industry.

It's Trojan time for boys
who wear it well,
i.e., the poisoned well
of Peloponnesian history,
all the noble lines
sung in verse no one recalls.

Decant the wine-dark words,
the open wounds, O muse!
Descant too long
and you'll abuse
the privilege of playing
hero at any stage of life
or death.

Each night the cloth's unraveled,
the story torn apart, and so
the blind man sees a way
to beat the crowd, to string the bow.

WRITER'S BLOCK PARTY

The world
on the other side
of this page
is clattering, messy;
boasts white churches,
city halls,
courts called to order,
libraries where books
obey decimals;
planes arrive
at destinations,
plain townsfolk enjoy
community.

On this side
the ink
is barely dry
when fear sets in,
words pull back
each of their letters,
subtracting lines
one by one,
retracting meaning
from the bottom up;
stories lack endings;
poems resemble
special pleading.

Here
we long for
that other side
where no one
is reading.

PIRATE

The name buzzes
my tongue
against my teeth

Ends with an open
pirate's
aahhr

Zanzibar

Once I beached
my dreams there

Walked back alleys
in Stone Town

There
the past
bleached out
all beauty
dark as a slave
washing Portuguese
laundry

One day
I defied
cobalt skies
and sapphire seas
to voice
jaundiced views
of history

TAKING OUT THE TRASH

The lesson's
not so much
the smell
or bother.

It's just
the fact,
the act:
you think
you're better
than this,
reduced
to a task
that's less than
you think
you should be
doing.

But the inner hauteur
is only as strong
as the Hefty
you haul
to the alley

to find
the Dumpster's full:

a warning
you're just
a truckful away
from the place
you could be
going.

CITY OF FICTIONS

Cleverness would suffice
for tenants on the Upper West.

If the subway gets the best
of you, then you'd better
not meddle with systems
even more clever than you.

Olmstead's ghost lobs acid
ripostes at those who would
trump his bucolic vision
of natural life in the city.

No pity for those who would
build something small
where tall cenotaphs stand
as revisions of history.

Primordial Atlas' shoulders
held the heavens, not earth,
earning winks from young lovers,
but shrugs from Rockefeller.

HERETIC

I'm the applauder
for the commander
I am the minion
of defeated dominions

I'm the cheap crack
shooting up the mirror
I am your seven years
of rehabbed sad luck

Drop me a dark line
for my snarling Clementine
I am the miner who
lost her to the brine

Remonstrate my fate
with a new cold war
I'm the chief of state
for old Thomas More

I am the poison
avenging the healthy
I'm the chosen one
to enrich the wealthy

WINGED VICTORY

Please watch your step:
the stairs are seemingly
endless. Yes,
something important
is missing.
But perhaps it's plausible
that the ship's prow,
fashioned in
(of all things) stone
is the only thing spared
the Manichean hand of time
and, of course, the British.
Far from home
she stands atop
an ocean of stone,
no head, no arms,
missing the trumpet
she held to announce
(wait)
(listen!)
the victory
of Greece
and art
over history.
Only this woman
and one of her hands
have ever been found
on Samothrace.
Here
you will see in her face
(yes! her face!)
an unearthly thrill,
cool triumph in her eyes.
And a moment from now
her wings will move
as she rises
to tour the Louvre,
and you will see
everything become
motion and grace.

LENT ET DOULOUREUX

I could look out the window.
I could feel anger well up in me
like the Great Flood of '93.
Farmhouses would come unseated
in the torrent of my blood
and course down my arteries.

I could sort through photographs.
I could see everyone I've ever known,
a manic slideshow in my brain
snapping every cell and neuron,
exploding memory with
resentment, disdain, contempt,
shutting down the cortex, amygdala,
blowing holes in my skull.

I could sit in a chair and think.
I could imagine my imagination
making sense of organs in my body,
heart, liver, spleen, kidneys,
lungs, stomach,
stuffed with years of
all I've known, felt, heard,
saw, thought, said,
not said.

I could listen.
I could hear the silence more clearly
than anything I've ever heard
or not heard
in this world.
Or the next.

A HISTORY OF THE COLONY OF RHODE ISLAND

I have sailed into Narragansett Bay to find you,
to hunt you down like a deer in a clearing,
no mercy in my heart, bitter iron after all these years,
to reclaim all that was lost, to level the blame;
you will recall: *Who is so safe as we, where none can do*
Treason to us except one of us two – a cold "Anniversarie."
I have visited the natives of Pocasset, I have talked
with Massasoit, who saw you teaching English,
who saw the deed you signed for land you did not own.
My ship *Revenge* made land at Aquidneck Island,
where Providence has granted me darkest foothold.
Beneath these waters, the remains of ancient settlements
and camps sway like seaweed in lethal currents,
washed away by the betrayal in your uncharted heart.
I say the road to Hell is paved with new inventions,
all of which I'll test on your soul – a stockade in the fort
I will burn around you, burn brightly around you –
an offering to the wounds that revoke my freedom daily.

MAPPLETHORPE'S DARKROOM

The photograph
turns substance
into counterpart

Unfinished images vanish
when pleasure discovers
tales without interlocutors

The focus must endure
conflicting remedies when
language patronizes contempt

Imagined police
enforce old laws
invented in nightmares

A shadow's memory
originates in a cave
light must enter, must illuminate

When the heart designs its sky
one revealing image
refuses dishonest love

ANTIPHON: INSTRUCTION OF THE FAITHFUL

Can instinct offend
any creature?

Can the animal outweigh
its dream?

Hindsight engages
personal anarchy

Fear misuses
memory's roots

Revolutionaries hack
unreported wrongs

The spirit recruits
perpetual song

INNOCENTIA ET USUS

1. Consolatio

The temperature will drop below freezing tonight
In that little heart of yours and

I will spread a tarpaulin over the lilac bush
To protect it from your destruction;

The hot young stud you lusted after
Will park his ass on your broken shoulder

To prevent you from destroying the apple trees
That Satan's snake requires to bring to an end

This sad simulacrum of paradise
Where we stupidly sit in the weeds

2. Disconsolatio

Breathless hands and calloused lungs
Won't take you anywhere when

Anywhere is where you think you're going
And even a handbasket is large enough

To transport all your broken bones
To a version of Hell you'd never recognize:

The hands, biceps, chest, lips, the brown eyes,
The quadriceps, calves, delts, the glutes;

Here the fires rage, here the pitchforks,
Here the forked tongue, the tail, sulfurous smoke

And every heavenless body you've lusted for
In your withered life that love has broken

AMADEUS

Is it possible to imagine being alive
As Mozart? Is it possible to imagine being

Inside the Allegretto of his Piano Concerto
No. 25, deep in the blinding illumination

Of the run of the notes, the unreal brilliance
Of the music that constantly poured through

The marvel of his head, hearing the notes of
The piano and then also the orchestra, your body

Moving like his body to the wild transfiguration
Of the world into sound as complex as the air?

Can you imagine, can you comprehend
Transforming this fragile life into the eternal?

LIGHTS OFF

The noiseless storm, the silent nightmare,
Jagged fracture, bone scraping bone, brittle

Pain unmatched by undelivered relief,
Death-defying hurt enmeshed deep in marrow

As bones collide and crumble, dissolve
As a useless narcotic in sparkling water,

Water that will never wash away the darkness
At the heart of every movement, every motion

To close debate and clear the messy record
Of every punch, every bruise, every knockout

Inflicted on this body, this head, these limbs
Gratuitously lopped off in tsunamis of hate

FIVE DOORS

I.

Not far off Boulevard Haussmann
near L'Opera, here, now,
the young man with the older man
seeks the secret, hidden door,
seeks a pulse that races far more,
faster than the breathless sprint through
the Métro to reach this portal before
fear and cowardice override
unashamèd lust. Then, behold, it opens.

II.

We could speak of Donatello
but where in the world would we be?
The door here seems Ghiberti's bronze
but isn't. Andiamo, let us go!
Much further south, in Firenze,
the hot, lithe men are sleek
and immeasurably discreet
even when they cast their eyes on heaven
while averting their eyes from hell.

III.

The perfectionist approaches the door
in sunswept, ancient Alexandria,
and he sees beyond it
men whose route to Ithaka
mattered less than the journey itself,
bejeweled, exquisite wandering
through sensuous touch, the lustrous skin,
unafraid of Laestrygonians or the Cyclops,
victorious at Thermopylae.

IV.

You, whoever you are, whose lilacs
in the dooryard bloomed into song
more alive and profuse than even the grass
on which your men recline,
men you nursed, to whom you gave new life:
we feel the bounding throb of your heart,
your body electric; we rest athwart your hip,
we hear your barbaric yawp, we hope,
we know, no love (your love) is unrequited.

V.

Permit us voyage, love,
into vast open lands where time
cannot erode those spindrift magical sands
on which you wrote the passions of your men,
bridged with the surly logic of metaphor, of semaphore.
The bodies you adored
are naked now, and free, smooth idioms
embodying your mythic god (O Dionysus!) in curveship
vaulting the welcoming harbor, the golden door.

ROSETTA

"and much room provided for
the wretched to find caves
to ponder way off in . . . "
-- A.R. Ammons

You who can see beyond
hieroglyphs which I
themselves cannot see

from you I have wanted
only I think
dry leaves to brush
dust away.

I have put
scratchings on hard stones.
I use weak points
metal unfit for men.

In this dark passage
I chip too quickly against
old dust flying
up in my face.

Shadows here process themselves
in my mind
between the light.
You've been watching behind
your light ghostly film

all this time I've wanted
what you cannot give,
what my new leaves
must find beyond fear
beyond scrawled darkness.

LEGEND

"But who will light
A legend that he will not celebrate?"
-- Philip Booth

Down to the dock
in Maine accents,
the descent to moorings, wood
urged to smoothness by sea and green weed,
the marvel here in setting forth
in fog, from hard and known land,
to places saved only by buoys.
You to the fore, I aft where the drone
of your motor dins close to me,
we head deep to waters I've not known
or cared for, leaving a wake the ocean
takes care of, seaming and smoothing
the waves back to clear, continuous form.

Here you have lived, from here
set forth, in fog sometimes
thicker than this, to break alone
into what it was
you found you were after,
some unmarked point of compass
or sextant, set low in morning,
distant, indistinct, new,
dim as sun through fog,
one place and that place's moment
unfathomed, unnamed.

Out now where language is
the gulls', wheeling white in mist,
your silhouette turns
at the stilled, unfractured line
the prow has marked;
you shadow me from the dawn's
unheralded halo.
You rise through that first light
and with skilled and certain hands
give to mine the dark, heavy iron,

sleek sinker knotted to worn hemp
like sea insurance.
Through your body, through
that need of all at sea

for markers in that awful wavering
whose margins always and
all ways roll away,
you tell me now to take it,
to heave it.
                                        A wand, it carries
the gleam of air down with it,
descending to where eventual settling
discerns the far, intangible bottom:
by the rope, so many fathoms
and so many off for drift.
Back through trying fingers,
the rope returns that cold
unfaltering amulet – medaled now
with its victory of sand – back
to the receptacle of your hands.
And there,
in climbing, widening light,
you give it to me,
this, the unimpartable gift.

TWO

Post Meridiem

"Now, as he worked for readers who lived in the shadows or might emerge into daylight in the future, he could use a tone that was hurt and hushed, and create an atmosphere as someone might light a vaulted space with candles."

-- Colm Tóibín, *The Magician*

MAKE

Make unknown words known
Make known words unknown
Make old words new

Make new words
new worlds

WHAT WE HAVE IN COMMON

The arc of justice disciplines
struggle

Defective imbalance lends us
disguise

The diameter of opinion measures our
wounds

Our bridges await the timed
explosives

My neighbor's apathy enlarges my
scream

Nerves sabotage the fireworks of
hope

We slap our asses with the nastiest
toy

Should a creed sneak into our secret
urge?

PROUT'S NECK, MAINE

I regret very much that I have painted a picture
that requires any description.
-- Winslow Homer

The beast imprisons rhetorical charm
Don't think only of the imagined wild
Imagine how epic wonder sweeps
over the white dance of salt spray

Take pride in the wet shouting
Let ignorance make a swan dive
Words overlap in the wind as
all swimmers take to the chase

Each beast assumes an implicit shape
Bright against the eastern shore
An appointed missile stalls in the air
Red sun darkens to a promised core

Divers swim against the rocks
Legs vouch for unknown ground
Accidents search for a warning
Bells startle their liquid sound

THE EARLIER WORLD

In the earlier world
an ambiguous desert
provokes unseen winter

One tree reigns as
our theological student
a remaining angel

Scripture calls for courage
A chapel hosts old heartache
A rough recruit ensures laughter

Even the defeated man
performs a calm drill
in lost fields of cotton

CAN YOU HEAR ME NOW?

Your devil rings
He corrupts every word from your mouth

Horror is supplemental to your understanding
You want to inflict a busy signal

You hang your eyes from a rusty nail
Every sound you make is a noisy sin

That brutal genius explodes bombs in your ears
His sensual weapons are aimed at your independence

With you he has met his quota

MY ELIGIBLE UNCLE

My eligible uncle trips into the corridor
His occupied width is thinner than air
His periphery attracts crisp appreciation
His void codes the wind for a public urge

A catastrophic paradise grows around him
Sun struggles to reach his curried body
His sphere of influence suffers all prejudice
His goal to avoid a sticky divorce

While marriage invites him from the start
Each time he manages an expensive escape
His companions speak from the alien corn
His closets are cleaner than ancient bones

LAKEHURST, NEW JERSEY

Secrets chart the soul against the heart
Hierarchies trick dangerous reporters with
undulating content destined for newsprint

Fluent passengers and the traveled boss
exchange their sorrows in voluminous air
The branded bull is enlarged with lust

How can the brain twist an unstable circle
while comfort stalls in hydrogen wind?
Ah, the sinful doubt and the doubtful sin.

MR. OPPENHEIMER'S REVENGE

Can a conscious likelihood
overlap doubt in any creature?
Favorable delight pools itself
in a hundred forgotten lives

A misunderstood sermon
calls for remarkable fruit
A snag unloads scientific tears
from tribes of failing executives

Can consequential truth multiply
into rows of asynchronous lies?
How does our own resemblance
stagger into the divine?

Polished anecdotes engulf
a provisional substitute's ascent
Cheers quickly stop when
the boys have a known departure

PROPAGATION OF THE FAITH

Mythology complements a cave
where gods are influential clients
who cheat at difficult recipes

God-police stalk the shores of Lethe
ticketing the wrecks of muscle cars
dictating epics to vestal virgins

Each one defects to the iron light
at a private Checkpoint Charlie
on the orders of deluded allies

They celebrate necessary lies
and solo jerk with bangled wrists
while terrorists sign on the dotted line

These gods reject our harsh religion
whose believers lunch on arrogant greed
Risible gospels mark a shameless breed

EVOLUTIONARY GRAMMAR

When will the damned assess
their changed circumstances?
When can the verbatim sea
overlook its flavored gerunds?

When does an essential god
spit like us in the bathroom sink?
Will a shy creator condemn
our earned place in the universe?

Beloved students mumble
in harsh evolutionary grammar
Their independence stretches
through a disorienting urge

How will an expanded god
clear a foolish conscience?
When will our bones prevent
the blackening of joy?

PHILOSOPHY OF MIND

The human body is the best picture of the human soul.
-- Ludwig Wittgenstein

1.
The prospective objective
induces the exclusive imperative

On a rural beach
refreshed teenagers slink
into practiced dives

2.
Why can't the heat oppose
a spike in the price of love?

Dear lover, let's lurk
in the exclusive imperative

3.
A deserving author
hides in his mailbox
to avoid expressing presence

Can language exit
with a cross word-puzzle?

4.
Below the water's surface
teenagers swim into
the prospective objective

Do you remember the day
you pretended to be
the exclusive imperative?

SUCKERED INTO THIS

In the sink we wash stray dogs
snatched from the floods of hell
When can a torturous drip mend?
Will a gusher eliminate misery?

A risky hotel collapses & synapses
in this modern myth of Sisyphus
A victim towers over the spirit
a kid chugging movie popcorn

Unsafe in a passionate neighborhood
we exchange deracinated frowns
Our dust portends distressing themes
Our rope assures a confidence scheme

INTERROGATORIES FOR A POWER OUTAGE

Will the unsuccessful dead
arise from the sea?
Should we empty our pockets
on the pliant sand?

Will permanent daylight
burn like antifreeze?
Shall we pour ourselves
blind against the shore?

Will tide pools struggle with
underground consequence?
Will unnamed phenomena
flood the earth?

Does the assumed center
intend to wobble?
Will our Ethernet hatred
shut down peace?

REPEALING THE BILL OF RIGHTS

Each driver resents the backseat passenger
A lyric genius pursues clawbacks in delight
Compulsory detectives write cheap pot-boilers
Drama queens seek storms to wreck the night

In our streets we bait the stimulated bulls
Our spokesman displays distressing reluctance
The supreme being ignores our shrieks
Our acting betrays a simplistic performance

The dead will deride our tolling bells
"This is not news so why do you say it?"
Because it frees our animals from zoos
Because it improves the optics of hell

As actors we nudge the subtlest meanings
We speak while fleeing a chorus of rats
Ask husbands when they stopped the beatings
Judges participate in our brutal attacks

NO ONE EXPECTS THE SPANISH INQUISITION

An intelligent lover spreads lies on the dock
Unlikely tongues laugh at purposeless books

The suffering defeated forgive lost battles
A riderless horse won't relinquish its saddle

Sinful gods sneak selfies on the newest iPhone
Chaos retreats into its red gelatin backbone

THE POWERFUL

The concerted word
can wield a hammer
Just did it

A jest will flower
among charmed birds
Tweeted that

Alcoholic ideals
compromise politicians
Dug that ditch

Flaws populate
the rarest fossil
Happens forever

Redefined rhymes
puzzle eyesight
Coax the blind

Moral hangovers
seek perfect hindsight
It's always 20/20

THE SEARCH FOR BLACK HOLES

The public incriminates anatomy
but always wants some ass
Flesh worries every harsh appraisal
then whistles at the farce

The newest universe disowns creatures
and ends its quest in smoking grace
Lovers rearrange their victims
to evade cold justice in inner space

THE IMPLACABLE MEETS THE UNMOVABLE

The lousy queen distracts the farmer
She lost her realm He lost his farm
They do not care for one another

Urges elaborate the rolling planet
Time and sex won't heal all wounds
Nothing will soften a life of granite

Contemporary fog surrounds the ancient
It soon will vanish in blades of sun
Timeless walls stand eternally patient

IT'S A SMUG RACKET

In the back room
amid cigar smoke
fat men in fedoras
rewrite insurance policies

When you dial
their unlisted number
the thinnest of them
lifts the black receiver

He has nothing to say
he merely listens maybe
for a minute maybe less
then hangs up

You were hoping
one of them perhaps
would answer a question
about life expectancy

EMERGENCY MANAGEMENT

Milk rains down
on this flooded town
faster than it can go sour

The local dairy
association
has some bottling issues

There's no way
dairymen can
keep up with this

In the big red barns
and local pet stores
cats are singing arias

MARCEL DUCHAMP MEETS SALVADOR DALÍ

You are finally steeped in
unpromised impersonal stress
So does enthusiasm suppress
your disappointing deed?

Your inhibited dependence
strives for epic harmony
You hum past mad musicians
drunk barbershop quartet

The eyes of every "secretary"
spin above their cheeks
proffering grim amazement
to plump drunken bosses

Your unexpected funeral
stimulates splendid killers
to polish the crazed surface
of your bald idiosyncrasies

THE PLAGUE

You wrap a stolen knife
around your disappointed wrist
No one will ever know
how the wall suffered your fist

You're such a handsome man
you're not a proverbial rat
You occupy that shabby place
where decent men once sat

But when citizens fear officials
they've bought into violations
as devious vermin always roam
where truth is no vocation

TOYS R LUST

Swimming pools
experiment with sunlight

Beautiful men
with languorous legs
in chaises longues
ponder unobtainable males

Boys turn another cheek
sopping wet
when they snap their Speedos

You could say
it's a Hockney

A glossy seal
claps and barks
in the shallow end

Glossy boys
talk and laugh

and cock their head
for the inevitable

math

RULES OF ENGAGEMENT

A star recovers defective light
The moon fails in a trembling fog
This floor withdraws in perfect spite

A dismal chord rattles a shell
Flowers dream in abundant grass
Redundant virtues ruin hell

Blackmail benches a wondrous quest
An evasive temper assumes disaster
A damaged household refuses guests

Susceptible lips refrain from lust
New fashions enrobe a mortal passion
The vast invisible guarantees our dust

TRUTHINESS

We're told but not convincingly
time will heal a sullen crush

We wear our bulletproof wisdom
like helmets of self-destructive kids

Behind a shed the state's attorney
plans rosy scenarios in black & white

He boasts of electoral freedoms
diminished by the rights of guns

DARK SECRET LOVE

Each of your deposits
in spiritual awakening
is booby trapped with hope

Gangs of juiced-up studs
hide their forbidden hard-ons
in the rafters of your rage

And now imagined fish
lie stranded on the beach
where waves erase

your damned innocence

THINGS YOU FORGOT

Supposed peace
adapts to violence

An untrue stream
reposes in pollution

The warble persists
in the dying bird

Instinct curses
the sophisticate

Relevance wastes
extravagance

No hero will take
center stage

A threshold vanishes
into a seed

DEMOS & POLIS

How does
an implausible variant
persist?
Will
the insufficient empire
survive its errors
without its laws?

Essential ancestors
patronize the saga
of base hypocrites
standardizing lies

That's when
the individual
dies

Red disaster
quibbles about
its murders

High-wire racists
normalize
their hijackings

Why
does the self
elect its own
worst enemy?

HUNTING HEAVEN

The connected door
worries the thought of height

The disinherited few
frantically glue
puzzle pieces
together

This is the way
the world
comes into view

We are hunting
heaven
cruising through
inhibiting light

Brilliance
unbearable
for human
sight

This pleasurable pain
sends a surprising invoice
for services surrendered

Men of the cloth
chafe at the collar
where the rope
will fit

DYSPASTORAL

The last grass
arrives
mysterious crop

A leaf rolls through each atom
The farmer spits
without significance

Unclear biology
engenders plague
striking down herds of aurochs

Bulls breed a hot dilemma
where terror is posted
to the world's last tree

Suppressed sod
becomes a carpet
for delirious dances in caves

Crickets bravely broadcast
the universe
in the fields where our mothers die

WAGGING FIVE DOG TAILS

1.
Can the sky
drown the universal?

When does a backspace
erase the eternal?

2.
A carefree method
becomes a discipline

3.
When money is no object
we wash the crystal in champagne

4.
Undecided students
overhear the anarchist

Horny boys in seminary
yearn to tongue the antichrist

5.
Does a critical tool
find its true purpose?

Does the poorest nightmare
awaken a billionaire?

THE WINDS OF MARTINIQUE

I.

Are we forever baffled by
the real?

II.

Bottled ego struggles
in its Caribbean adventures
to the last resort
on sun-bleached beaches
where tourists reach
the end of their dope
the last of their stash
the bottom of hope

III.

Hope is a pool
all souls hurry
to swim in
drown in
be found in
settle down in
astound in
be unbound in

IV.

We dry off in lies

We won't be tied down
in what's true
to the meaning
of the unreachable few

V.

The visible is reversed
in the mirror of insight
where flesh seeks pleasure
in a lost resort

VI.

Far off in the bay
dolphins play
in the funeral of reality

REGARDING RERUM NATURA

Should symbols reason with intrinsic patterns?
Should they stand alone?
Discreetly dial an iPhone?
Fold their spirits around moons of Saturn?

Can chaos recognize a suicide?
Can it perform its own?
Or, instead, eat its own?
Sheepishly repay a loan?

Why does the wish hesitate? Or meditate?
The desire obfuscate?
Or iron nerve oscillate?
The longing fail to belong?

Must second thoughts check the whim?
Or science explain mysterious wonder?
Or fear multiply every blunder?
Or silence at last engulf the hymn?

SIX ESSENTIALS FOR THE UNINITIATED

1.
The forest
is innocent

The tale
is guilty

2.
Biochemistry won't
build an ego

The hog never assures
a healthy meal

3.
An unwelcome god
bothers a weed

Engineers adjust
hazy potential

4.
Impulsive strength
fathers anger

A badge triumphs
behind a bullet

5.
Half ownership
throws dice

Every footnote
lies to a crowd

6.
The poem doubles
a great drum

THE TALENTED VISITOR

Bright memory
leans against
the earliest variant
of truth

which is beauty

which leans against
a piece of everyday
painted crockery
brought from the kitchen
belowstairs

On the silver salver
on the mahogany table
in the silent front hall
lies the ghostly card
of Mr. Keats

Elsewise

the Hampstead house
is unremarkable
and completely still

In the garden
however
the local nightingale
is secretly preparing
to make this evening
difficult for sleep

VITA BREVIS BUT ARS NO LONGA

Virtue sleeps above the wind
(the wind's virtue is zephyrous)

It knows
art is
the sixth sense
the fifth element
the eighth wonder
the fourth member
hiding in the trinity

Rising dreams reference the prophet
the prophet beholds the icy planet
the planet roams among dark strangers
the strangers evaporate in rising dreams

The virtuous obliging moon
sleeping above the wind
is always
the lamp to our feet

UPPER PALEOLITHIC NOTES

The ear
unwinds
        a short
        song
across a flute

The song
retrieves
a corner of
        its origin
wherein
        something
        inside
        becomes
sound
through
intervention
of invention

Nothing
        can take
its place
in a dark space

Holes
        carved into
bird bone
        roll back
the night

The bone
carries
        shafts
        of music

sound now
in flight

channels
of light

VIKING TOURS

Discontinued wind
pauses over a disturbance
at the sharp peak of midnight

The unobtainable secret
shows its rigid wrists to
tourists in their cultural urges

A shot of coincidence
makes its triple loop
into consequential postcards

In daylight why won't flesh
recognize wild organic lust
disguised as complicated prayer?

Balance is abandoned portside
while acculturated swords swing
against conventional arrivals

NEW FRAGMENTS FROM HERACLITUS

Beneficial desires
lust for loose collars

The greatest mimic
waits near a skull

The heated planet
curtails the incapable

A follower
heels strange independence

A patient cat
will see paradise

BELIEVE IT OR NOT

I.
Nothing puzzles the devil
No bullet discriminates

No hero seeks headlines
The phoenix defies its origins

No mortal shadow
can purge its ghost

II.
The moon slowly cruises around joy
while innocent glory quickly skips town

Paint repairs the angry moment
Deep injury empties philosophy

III.
Peace detains the general
Even the universe strays

IV.
A well fancies a victim

QUANDARY QUARTET

1.
An inverted birth
and meaningless anomalies
perplex unhappy bishops

2.
A hovering island
lifts its shadow
to rebuke the sea

3.
Coarse sailors raise
their disciplinary oars
to rip the epic flood

4.
Suspicion once opened
stirs the reflexive beast
egged on to solo victory

STUDENT ORGANIZING COMMITTEE FOR PEACE

An imagined ghost surfaces outside the stiff body
His eyes freeze in the physics of the defeated

Drunks boast expertise in incomprehensible circles
Their winded companions slip into minimal rhyme

The beginning student stumbles on moral realms
Her immeasurable thoughts explore a slice of justice

Exploding chords send time into slippery streams
Afternoon conjecture ends a gorgeous credendum

Prayers of gold won't repair the nearest human error
Brave students talk across cold ink to visualize the air

NOTES TOWARD UNKNOWN TRUTHS

Suppressed hope presses
against the throat

A priest lightly evaluates
addictive faith

Needles slide into
forgotten injuries

Lost champagne triggers
warming laughter

The potential represents
the symptom

The bankrupt despair
before anger expires

Fuming instinct sparks
interior fireworks

Should the brain kidnap
aggressive skin?

A sweeping comparison
will bloat the ego

Sunlight advances
even ungrateful trees

NEAR SCATTERED PRAISE LIES OUR SUBSTANTIAL ENDEAVOR

1.
Lucky soil
next to a lazy stream
relaxes in the shade

An echo in
the world's last canyon
flows in spreading pleasure

2.
A dark wolf
scratches the fears
of every sentinel

Jealous rivals
reject abundant crops
ready for the harvest

3.
A cobbler's son
dreams of cheating chance
in a leather palace

Old doctors
see waste pulsing
within the vein

EXPLICATION DE TEXTE

Commentators advance fancied complaints
in demanding footnotes
unwilling to fold into bankrupt silence

An empty glance and a drooling cheek
exceed all propaganda
to frustrate disturbing freedom

The unread body presses attacks
where invented hypotheses reign
and radicals snack on brilliant crystal

A massed choir groans at headlines
favoring the fully flown truth
defined and declined in raining dismay

HIS WORTHY GOD

Delight sings past its inherent midnight
Dinner on top of the delicious world

Time itself awaits swift inauguration
Steadfast fidelity orbits sublunar earth

An observer safeguards frail eyesight
Expensive decadence disaffects all air

Inner force rages against external math
Let upward blindness storm into prayer

Fragments and Petites Essais

THE RAINBOW ROOM

★

The bold foreigner
underestimates his map

★

Why can't the impractical nugget
make a perfect heart of gold?

★

Synonyms argue as if
saying the same thing

★

The god is drunk inside his temple

★

Why can't a mouse prompt the heavens?
When won't the devil offend?

★

An eternal wrist sports a tennis bracelet

TARWATHIE

★

The swallow dances with the crescent moon

★

Decay hesitates around physical delight

★

A human defines the earth
How can its biology blackmail the blessed?

★

The sea risks losing the whale

★

The valley pretends to weigh the heights

CARTHAGE

★

Can empires triumph in ordinary prose?

★

Childhood amounts to needless horror

★

Will a workload manufacture
a real intellectual?

★

Adrift in flawed acceptance

★

In even the slightest epic
birth intervenes

★

Rocks polish love
in each new paradise

TIMES SQUARE

★

The changing century laughs at history

★

Blank chapters of empty defeat
win a six-figure advance

★

A virgin reassures her chauffeur

★

Modern misfortune suspects history

★

The lunatic bums a smoke from a suicidal god

★

The specific noun fears
a reverse dictionary

★

The worst marriage plays
an anniversary game

★

In the upper house of ignorance
justice thanks a wary verdict

★

Dreams in practiced beds
reason with seas of compromise
before the arriving dead

★

A fence halts the fire burning in our fields
In the garden glass men bowl with oranges

THÉÂTRE DE BABYLONE

★

Disregarded advice rumbles through the night

★

Pieces of the past migrate to new addresses
The future sends texts to warn the present

★

Can faith hurt?
Does the toad create the prince?
Will grammar enforce comprehension?
Does impending anger bless its axe?

★

Vertical accidents trip in the head
the ego reasons where angels tread

★

A cancelled prophet
rants throughout the village

★

Youth hunts thirsty passion
with baffled lips

★

Can this charmed earth
shake off memory's receipts?

★

Silence moans within romantic lovers

★

Ink interferes with an eloquent white expanse

RADCLIFFE CAMERA

★

High in the alphabetical palace
mortal flesh deceives decay
Song triumphs against anarchy

★

We learn outside of school
that every lock can be unlocked

★

Can biochemistry
prevail against
the muck?

★

Hierarchy sips
an oppressed champagne

★

Do words
bring ideas?
Do ideas
bring words?

★

Why can't the problem change?
A trusting heart

★

Each lie
an ally
washed with cash

LA CAÑADA FLINTRIDGE

★

The parrot snacks behind its green charm

★

Restrained impulse
bores intelligence

★

Processed hate
fears satire

★

Desire highlights the unknown
The ego spins
through reckless thirst

★

Revenge invites an uneasy owner

★

Luxury swallows hindsight
Bliss ignores a prayer

★

Sarcasm skips through genetics

★

A punishing creator
rivals a careless lecturer

CHÂTEAU DU CLOS LUCÉ

★

Anatomy emerges from a song
licensing the fiddle
as stars signal regret

★

Gravity boils under biology

★

Grief powers transformation

★

Marriage incinerates independence
A child inhabits your emergency

★

Can the sacred prison create an artist?

★

Ritual faith rejects all queries

★

The species is wedded to mystery

LINCOLN CENTER PLAZA

★

Does the astronomer cry over paradox?
Every mortal must hear the exceptional cheer

★

Prayer accounts for the grave

★

Trouble's farther cousin
multiplies under your breath

★

Our windows dance to celebrate
approximate virgins at the barre

★

Discipline mends punishing wounds
drawn through unfamiliar sleep

★

Theory meets appearances
Appearances cheat theory
A happy romance repairs intercourse
trusting reasonable therapy

WINDOWS ON THE WORLD

★

Wisdom decides constraints
but laws will always discriminate

★

Defeated grace frees the soldier
beneath the killing god

★

Unsupported magic
begs every rabbit

★

Will inhibited desire
think?

★

The rainbow strips away
its spectrum

★

Licensed language drags its ink

★

His concerned ego adjusts the curtains

★

A trifle aborts the universe

★

Sure hope rocks every chart
balancing ancient sound

★

The supreme voice resides in undefined pain

SOUTH WOODLAWN AVENUE

★

Our mental life smokes at every lunch

★

Capitalism is seated with a non-consenting adult

★

Promising historians
divulge repetitive ignorance

★

Ecological midnight
captures the primitive

★

The welcome wallet mothers a paying insight

★

A debatable god reasons behind your garage

★

Laughter ghosts the gorgeous sexist

★

When will a prefix differentiate the universal?

GRASMERE

★

A prize dances around its defects

★

Capital crime resides in the soul

★

A nun will razor a prayer

★

Boredom sings in pure symmetry

★

Misery rules psychology
and crashes in narrow streets

★

Heaven patiently waits for the natural supernatural

★

Can forests intervene with nameless nature?
Will the spoken heart wall off our silent words?

★

Old misfortune
tolerates its brother

★

Patience doubles as the millionth winter
Sobriety rages inside fermented cider

VIA ZAMBONI

★

How can the damned improve their comfort?

★

When censorship condenses the mob
fever strikes the electorate

★

A breach in revelation beckons toward heaven
privileged with the shaken gospel

★

Thought achieves a roof
Reluctance dances inside a kiss

★

Drastic enthusiasm
studies the ballet

★

The concealed shape
behind the faithful guitar
slips into a dream
of soundless freedom

★

Error rents suspicious adjectives

★

Shapeless hatred
flips burgers at the local joint

MISSION SAN JUAN BAUTISTA

★

The forgiving heart
bends like a straw
soothes the burning eye
masters the grave's silence

★

The documented soul
cleans its windows

★

The stair must invest in sky

★

An answering glue
stops history's clock

★

Faith has a license to print money

★

How wisely a demon will procrastinate

★

Every phoenix inherits
the implausible

★

Does the criminal profile the police?

★

An obliging keeper assures a tidy zoo
but cannot guarantee who's eaten
ordered off the menu

★

The cynic misinterprets
a call for volunteers

"Countdown" was published in the following publications: *Inside Outer Space: New Poems of the Space Age,* an anthology edited by Robert Vas Dias (Doubleday, 1970); *How Porcupines Make Love: Notes on a response-centered curriculum,* edited by Alan C. Purves (Xerox College Publishing, 1972); *Reality in Conflict: Literature of Values in Opposition,* Edmund J. Farrell, et al. (Scott, Foresman, 1976); *The Writing Process: Composition and Applied Grammar,* Miles C. Olson, et al. (Allyn and Bacon, 1982); and *On the Wing: American Poems of Air and Space Flight,* edited by Karen Yelena Olsen (University of Iowa Press, 2005).

"On Nearing the Isle of Ithaca" and "Doing Laundry" were published in *Story: The Yearbook of Discovery,* 4th series, edited by Whit and Hallie Burnett (Four Winds Press, 1971) [Story College Creative Awards Contest of 1970-1971].

ABOUT ATMOSPHERE PRESS

Atmosphere Press is an independent, full-service publisher for excellent books in all genres and for all audiences. Learn more about what we do at atmospherepress.com.

We encourage you to check out some of Atmosphere's latest releases, which are available at Amazon.com and via order from your local bookstore:

Until the Kingdom Comes, poetry by Jeanne Lutz
Warcrimes, poetry by GOODW.Y.N
The Freedom of Lavenders, poetry by August Reynolds
Convalesce, poetry by Enne Zale
Poems for the Bee Charmer (And Other Familiar Ghosts), poetry by Jordan Lentz
Serial Love: When Happily Ever After... Isn't, poetry by Kathy Kay
Flowers That Die, poetry by Gideon Halpin
Through The Soul Into Life, poetry by Shoushan B
Embrace The Passion In A Lover's Dream, poetry by Paul Turay
Reflections in the Time of Trumpius Maximus, poetry by Mark Fishbein
Drifters, poetry by Stuart Silverman
As a Patient Thinks about the Desert, poetry by Rick Anthony Furtak
Winter Solstice, poetry by Diana Howard
Blindfolds, Bruises, and Break-Ups, poetry by Jen Schneider
Songs of Snow and Silence, poetry by Jen Emery
INHABITANT, poetry by Charles Crittenden
Godless Grace, poetry by Michael Terence O'Brien
March of the Mindless, poetry by Thomas Walrod
In the Village That Is Not Burning Down, poetry by Travis Nathan Brown
Mud Ajar, poetry by Hiram Larew
To Let Myself Go, poetry by Kimberly Olivera Lainez
Saints of Sacred Madness, poetry by Joyce Kessel

ABOUT THE AUTHOR

Ronald J. Penoyer was born in Syracuse, NY in 1951. He earned a bachelor's degree from Cornell University, *magna cum laude*, and a master's degree from Johns Hopkins University, both in English and American literature. At Cornell he studied with A.R. Ammons, M.H. Abrams and others; at Hopkins he studied with Hugh Kenner, Donald R. Howard and others. At Exeter College, University of Oxford, he studied early Twentieth Century English literature. He worked as a researcher, writer and editor at a public policy research center at Washington University in St. Louis, where he edited or co-wrote policy studies with the economist Murray L. Weidenbaum and others. He also held executive positions at St. Louis companies for 32 years, first with Ralston Purina Company, then with Boatmen's Bancshares and FleishmanHillard Inc. For much of his adult life he played the tenor, alto and soprano saxophones.

Other publications by Mr. Penoyer include the following: *Reforming Regulation of Hazardous Waste* (CSAB, 1985); *Labor Relations in Transition: Bankruptcy Law vs. Labor Law*, co-editor with Kenneth W. Chilton (CSAB, 1984); *The Next Step in Regulatory Reform: Updating the Statutes*, with Murray L. Weidenbaum (CSAB, 1983); *Toward a More Open Trade Policy*, with Murray L. Weidenbaum and Michael C. Munger (CSAB, 1983); *Making the Clean Air Act More Cost-Effective*, with Kenneth W. Chilton (CSAB, 1981); and the *Directory of Federal Regulatory Agencies* (CSAB, editions in 1978, 1980, 1981).

(Photo credit: A.J. Lenrope)

Made in USA - North Chelmsford, MA
1327311_9781639884896
08.16.2022 1412